Puppies In and Out

Linda Ekblad

Toronto

Five puppies on a rope pull and play.

One puppy goes away.
How many puppies stay?

Four puppies stay to play.

Five puppies go to swimming school.
Two puppies leave the pool.
How many are left in swimming school?

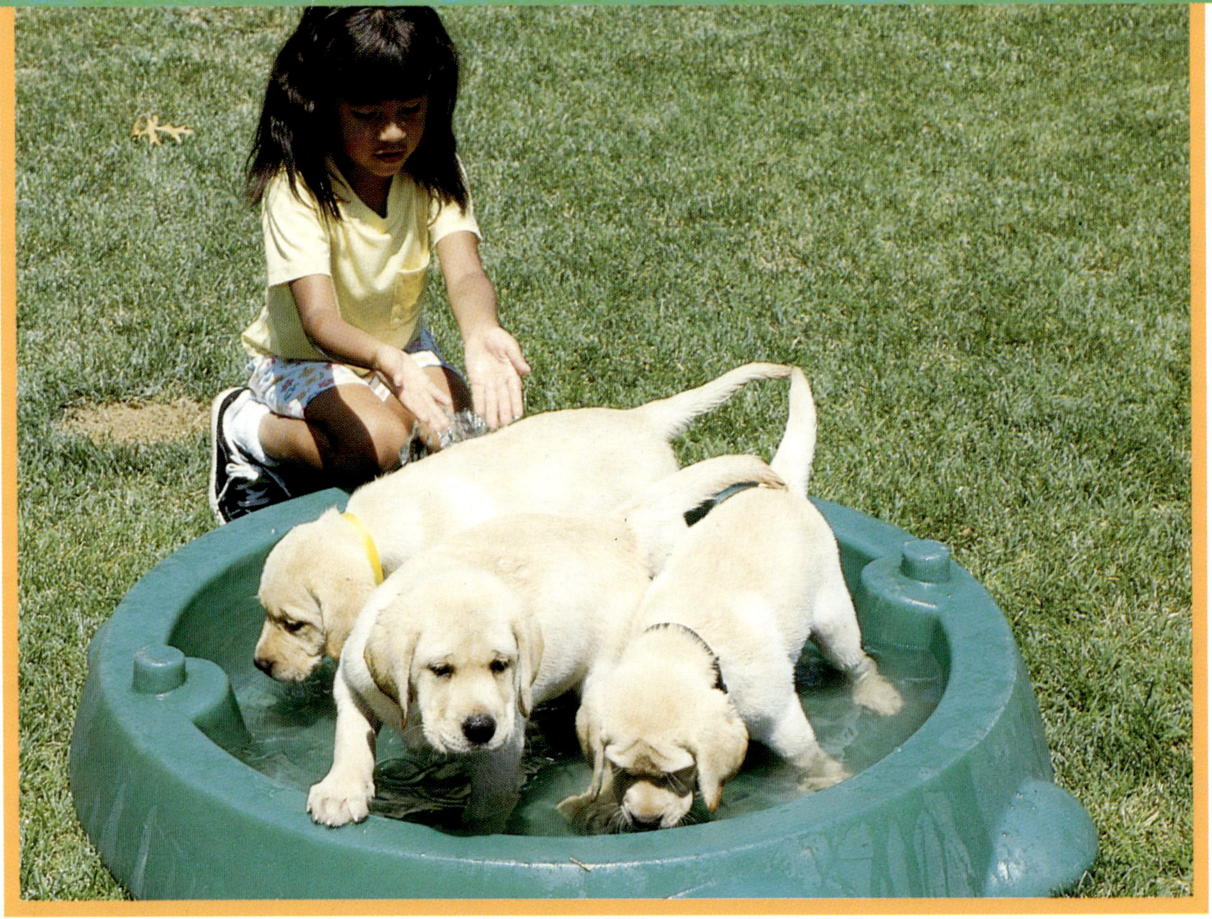

Three puppies are left in the pool.

Five puppies sit in their bed.

Three puppies stay in bed.
How many puppies play instead?

Two puppies go to play instead.

Five puppies run and play.

Four puppies run away.
How many puppies stay?

One. What a day!